ASCENT OF THE MOTHERS

Noelle Kocot

WAVE BOOKS

Ascent of the Mothers

SEATTLE & NEW YORK

Published by Wave Books

www.wavepoetry.com

Copyright © 2023 by Noelle Kocot

Wave Books titles are distributed to the trade by

Consortium Book Sales and Distribution

Phone: 800-283-3572 / SAN 631-760X

Library of Congress Cataloging-in-Publication Data

Names: Kocot, Noelle, author.

Title: Ascent of the mothers / Noelle Kocot.

Description: First edition. | Seattle : Wave Books, [2023]

Identifiers: LCCN 2023009906 | ISBN 9781950268870 (paperback)

Subjects: LCGFT: Poetry.

Classification: LCC PS3611.036 A73 2023 | DDC 811/.6—dc23/eng/20230301

LC record available at https://lccn.loc.gov/2023009906

Designed by Crisis

Printed in the United States of America

9 8 7 6 5 4 3 2 1

First Edition

Wave Books 112

FOR JO-ANN SLEIGHT, LIZZETTE POTTHOFF,
AND AGNES ELIZABETH WHITESIDE
AND TO THE MEMORY OF DEAN YOUNG

ASCENT OF THE MOTHERS

LABYRINTHITIS

A
Small
Ocean
Inside
The
Head
Outside
The
Waters
Are
More
Choppy
Triggered
By
Acute
Spiritual
Experiences
I
Get
Dizzy
As
A
Saint

Or
A
Bumbling
Human
Being
I
Could
Swear
I
Saw
A
Star
Fall
Out
Of
My
Hair
Once

Nut's edge, crabgrass, it's all
So reliable like lessened happiness.

The fact of a neck, craning outward
To survey the damage. Like a curtain

On the air, a narrative without a photograph.
I am thinking you are alive again,

And I put your picture in with the warmth
I hold. I could never rest, the mouth

Of the word keeps me up nights.

FLOWERS

Lucent transitions, the heat
And draft of four stories, how did
I get here so quickly? My attention
Always wavering, as my eye wanders

In and out of apprehension. Give
Me one reason I shouldn't be scared?
I tell you this: that down comforter
Is a tent by the waters of Babylon,

And I do what I do without complaint
Now. The beautiful minimum by the
Drunken window, something for just
Myself for a little while. Throat held

Up to the moonlight, the silver of
Spring evenings, they're flowers, they know.

THE PHYSICAL WORLD

This is where we live. The green
Grass sways, I sway, too. That which
Is barely audible still makes a slight
Sound. The phosphorescence of cities,

The long tongue of evening licking the
Wind. This stairstep, that doorknob,
The undercurrent of history making itself
Larger. How we inhabit the music,

How the music is a fish with its mouth
Open, golden coins spilling everywhere.
This is not what I came here for, but I will
Remain without revising. I have one

Windowpane filled with smoke marks,
The other as damp as a stack of rags.

DIVINATION

Let's be God
For a moment,

Shall we?
That which invites

Composition,
That which is suspended

From a great height,
The presence

Of approximation
Heavy in the meadows,

I'm not afraid,
And yet

My shroud vanishes
In these lines,

I am so wept
Past weeping,

And what seems to hold
The world in its place

Is evidence of the
Weighted trees,

And leaves me always
Wanting.

THE ANIMALS

The warmest winter storm now over,
My splendid chamber all in disarray.
As I go on inventing myself, as the
Audience is fewer and fewer, I would

Say I was struck by memory, and the
Haze of what swells and collapses, nothing
But grace and a few lines to form a shape.
The opera's pulse, a flower left out for

Us. The undulant doves carrying messages
In their mouths, number upon number
Of slow and patient animals. How selfless
They are, and how loving, living in perfect

Fulfillment with their precise expressions
Of tireless faith, wishing us all so well.

GEORGE BAILEY

Beauty is your liquid shoulders.
Beauty is the cat.
Beauty is the plant who dies
And resurrects.
Beauty is the whole damn sun.
Beauty, which escapes me now,
Is a Tuesday as green as a summer leaf.
Beauty welcomes us onto the stage,
And we are awkward or content.
Beauty, you are mine, and I will go
With you into the gelid night
And lasso the moon like George Bailey.

I pray to be strong
Like the ox, or like the ant
Carrying two ants.

BEFORE A SHOWER

I envy myself—
That beige lump

Of flesh,
Boop boop booping around

Like a little ball
Of joy!

DRUNK

Amplitudes of sunlight, the incongruous
Night. See me looking in that window,
Bereft, drunk, wasting all my time. Here,
My garden is thinning, the blue shadows

Of the sky on the deck in twilight. What
Longs for spirit is only a body. I would
Say anything to have one, again, again.
There's nothing that's mine here, and I

Travel so light. The moon huge, the new
Blooms opening by faith. Drunk, I slept
On the stairs, and the mercury lamps flared between
Worlds. What pushes toward the future,

What grows without us, this is what I want,
And a few birds on a dock, the unfathomable water.

AT THE HOME

Living separately now, it's
As if we can barely even speak.
The wheelchairs whizz by
Like fireflies in a sea of gray hair.
Some smile. Some look on
Blankly. For some, dying is
Taking all their attention.
You will come home to my dinners
And the glow of fall evenings.
You are my precious one,
The one who stands at the lamppost,
Light turning to amber
Around your shaking face.

INSTRUCTIONS FOR THE WIND

Your loping voice,
The old cadence inhabiting

Anywhere.
On the dark pavement,

A red wing lies.
We who doubtless think

We are immortal
Sit here at the riverbank

While a sidewalk full of icons
Grows cold.

SONG OF COVID-19

We are here. The endless
Monologues, the trees in their beds.

I want to add that nothing
Is touching me.

I want to add that in the hallway
Filling with noises,

I greet you. You are so soft
And tender when I touch you.

But wait, I don't touch you,
I haven't touched anyone for months.

I hear you in the music, raining now.

MIGRAINE

Two of every naked animal—
Sheets of water,

Stuck nests and lawns,
Your animated face in my hands,

Studded with cigarettes
And then someone recognized us.

Two of every animal
Inside my head.

CRYSTAL GAYLE

My mother picks her arm
Like a gorilla
Searching for lice

*

I am stable now,
But the world is not.

*

I go to see my trees
In the mornings—
Horace, Rothgar, Hildegaard,
Piney, Tall, Barney, Fred, Wilma,
Pebbles, George, Elroy, Astro,
Frau Starr and Goethe.
They are part of my family.

*

Trump ding ding dings
On television
As I dump the wastebaskets.
Getting cold again.
Nine months of this.

*

Theology interests me
And aliens.

I don't know what to make
Of either.
And oh, the books about mosses.
I wish I were in North Carolina now,
But there is no chance of that.

*

I thought a lot about how
My father tried to murder me,
How I ruined my teeth
With bulimia.

*

I lost my job
Because a consulting firm
Told them to cut my classes out.
Students said they did not
Commit suicide
Because of my classes.

*

I'm fed up with the world,
But I love it all the same.

*

I've had a lot of time to think.
Thinking is not dangerous.

*

I need to rest now,
As I've been staying up nights
For no particular reason.
Mosses gather
Around my legs in dreams,
And the city seems far behind.

*

The light on my skin is bright
And unforgiving.
I need a haircut,
Or maybe I don't.
Maybe I'll let my hair grow
Down to my knees
Like Crystal Gayle.

A FISH

Tough shit in the wilderness! I need
Some guidance about those fucking
X-rays. Donna won't help. I watch
The clock turn to 1:11. I wrote the

Great American novel last night. Everything
Is shattered, everything is breathing.
The city is impossible with all of its wind.
It was in the eyes that carried us. Penelope

Went zigzag all over the place. Let me
Live on the arc of things yet to come. I
Totaled the car. Just kidding! Like a
Question that blows lucky into a steamboat,

Like a blurred flare over my essence slipping
Away, I am no longer human, but am a fish
Caught in a net. All I do is take up space
On the holes, all I do is wipe my bloody mouth on silence.

DELRAN

Your supple shoulders, your right to
Be more dead than you ever were. What
Is this sunlight, glaring over the Hudson?
What is this oil and kerosene on the inland

Lamps? It's anybody's guess. The night
Ferry comes, the slouched wind over the
Dock. Now we move to a forest, trees
Bending in the wind but not breaking. There

Is something to this resilience we find, and
Even with the noon before us, the corner
Mailbox is inconsolable with lack of letters.
What could not go on without us, the hidden

Places in fulfillment of experience. How happy
We were that day, driving to Delran. We must
Lose ourselves in the indecipherable, we must
Not care that we are living, and hum to a lighter voice.

POEM FOR MY GODDAUGHTER HANNAH

The intractable landscape, the harsh sun
On our faces. Waves of *we're alive*. Whatever

Happens to me. Silhouette of winter on
The clock hands. Humans aren't doves. You

Could be anyone today, have I ignored you?
Driven, though recognizable, encountering

Something you lost along the way. There is
A stubborn thing that does not diminish. In

The late afternoon, an angular verb makes
Us whole. A lone leaf transfixes the air.

Ascetic, and the endless
Gestures.

There is no time like now
To live,

And I think it is simply
The best I could.

Atmosphere perfectly
Timed,

A lot of drama and upset,
But I stand

In the middle of it,
Recklessly learning

The curve and chance
Of a studied approach.

Don't get austere, stay
As baroque as touch,

While the next morning
Rears its head,

And the sparrows say
Their peace.

I was beautiful once.
I have that to my name

And now, what is acceptable
To me

Shines forth, and I am able
To be an embarrassment,

And a candle flame
To those who are hum

And cover
For a reach to the gusts

Of wind from a window
Or a door.

GRAVELY LISTENING

Tag of a prayer,
Fixed accident of the fog,

The silence-seed
Is the mimicry of exhaustion.

Yes, I have wasted my life,
But so what?

Wake and shadow
Of the invisible,

The ones you can see
Make out like bees.

SALVATION

The long rain, the hungry
Ghost. I am watching something

Fall. The newspaper said
Something leisurely

Today, and I scanned it
Twice to look for your

Image. Nothing's here.
Soon I will no longer be

One big self, and what
Will happen to me? Let go.

Vanity is so yesteryear,
And I am not a fallen hero.

The unglazed windows,
An afterthought out of perspective,

This is what's left,
Something difficult, a fragment.

ASCENT OF THE MOTHERS

Glorious tripod
Of a million years,

Faces and draft,
Days not uncommon

Where my eye wandered.
Ruined clothes,

Heaps of cars
Over a stray's splayed paws.

I am nothing,
Or else I have made myself

Too big for words.
Take my hands,

There. Now the winter
Light steeps the nerve of it.

SAY IT

Audience of the moment—
The old story.

So what's the use of sleep?
The fall grass surges.

I'll tell you what I mean—
The margins inherit

Something dark and alert,
The hurry of leaves

Turning to (say it) rose.

When will I stop punishing
Myself for that?

Birds know how
To fly in formation,

Composers know how
To write nocturnes,

And here I sit, a shiver
Of light

With a moment's pure
Mutable

Starry voice.
The candles wink,

And I know that a million
Times

I long to be a soul,
And yet,

My body slogs on
Past all history

And unfettered
Atmosphere.

LETTER TO ELI

The long haul there,
The exigencies.

The pregnant women mutter
Something I can't hear.

The salt tide
Watching us go down,

What's left of something difficult
To understand.

My tears stain
A sheet of news.

I am excluded,
Yet I am not the center of everything.

An object chiming
In the far distance,

The raked lawns and choked
Noises of my fugitive heart,

The glow of evenings
At the end of July,

My possible future,
Its breezy blur.

What is it that I am
Assenting to?

The voyeur in the tale,
The beast in

The kitchen,
The roots of grass

Cry out.
Affection gone awry,

The violins begin
And end.

I am an exhaustion
And a vanishing,

And yet I stand here
Cold as day,

And tell you, the things
Of this world

And their meanings
Ring more perfectly

When done for nothing
And no one.

Far wind chimes a tree. A
Steep fire

Brews. That night it
Snowed,

There was only kindness.
Now, unguarded,

There is something
I can't know,

But know.

OUT OF HIDING

Lavish sky, utterance.
Though evidence

Suggests
I am singular,

I beg to differ.
How happy they seem

Over there!
Fulfillment of a watery

Sphere,
Life seems like lead

At times,
And the weight I carried

Was nearly frozen.
We lose ourselves

In iridescence.
The one soul is a cipher,

The other,
A future flame.

The trees humming, everything
Humming, and the wall

Which blankly holds you up
Is what makes me think.

Thought steers from its course,
And the future is

Nothing detectable.
I'm afraid of sleep.

You are no little one anymore,
Yet you are awake

And young and there are
Terrific reasons

For your presence.
How heavy life became,

And then you spoke bewildered
And unguarded

Into the July air.
I didn't know what to do,

So I just stayed there
And watched you turn into

A hermit crab
In your blue stroller.

Now, you are going away,
All goodness in tact,

And I only from a distance
Shelter your wild form.

THERE IS DARKNESS
OVER THE LAND

Sitting on the deck at
Twilight,

The moon dropping
Its red shadows

On the geometry
Of us,

The physical ash
Of sleep

Comes on again.
How soon will I

Submit myself
To another test,

Glad to talk
To those who

Aren't yet dead.

DISASTERS

It
Is
June
No
May
No
April
And
The
Intransigent
Birds
Go
On
With
Their
Chirping
And
The
Many
Disasters
Which
Overtook
Me

Seem

Fractured

Into

A

Greater

Whole

I

Do

Not

Mind

Them

Nor

Even

Care

Today

I

Just

Want

To

Stay

In

This

Refracted

Sunlight

And

Think
About
Nothing
In
Particular

ACKNOWLEDGMENTS

Grateful acknowledgment is made to the following publications where some of my poetry appeared: *The American Poetry Review*, *Juke*, *SurVision Magazine*, *Conduit*, *New American Writing*, and *The Poetry Review*.

I would also like to give heartfelt thanks to the following individuals: Charlie Wright, Barb Wright, Joshua Beckman, Matthew Zapruder, Anthony McCann, Matthew Rohrer, Heidi Broadhead, Catherine Bresner, Izzy Boutiette, Jeff Clark, Blyss Ervin, my parents, Jo-Ann and Jack Sleight, Dean Young, Denise Duhamel, Franz Wright, Mary Ruefle, Sandra Simonds, Allison Joseph, CAConrad, Laura Cronk, all of my teachers, students, and prayer partners, Milou, Damon Tomblin, Ivey Williams, Lizzette Potthoff, Sören Potthoff, Hannah Potthoff, Jochen Wachter, Paul Vlachos, Tonya Morton, Sheri Oshinsky, Isaac ben Ayala, Curtis McCartney, Cindy Cuarino, Stephanie Horn, Agnes Elizabeth Whiteside, Jane Brady-Close, Steve Berg, Elizabeth Scanlon, Rachael Allen, William Waltz, Anatoly Kudryavitsky, Andrew Fried, Carol Kiyak, Paul Hoover, Mayor Griffin and town council, and my dear sis, Monica Antolik, the animals, the trees, and anyone I am forgetting. May everyone be continually blessed and happy on this journey!! Thank you all so much!!